Wayne
The
Wombat

Making Friends

Margaret Kamla Kumar
Laila Savolainen

U
ma
Publishing
Group

NATIONAL
LIBRARY
OF AUSTRALIA

A catalogue record for this book is available from the National Library of Australia

ISBN: 978-0-6454789-9-0 (paperback)
ISBN: 978-0-6458192-1-2 (hardback)
ISBN 978-0-6458192-0-5 (ebook)

This book is part of the: Kashy Koala Series
Author: Margaret Kamla Kumar
Illustrator: Laila Savolainen

Interior / Cover / Artwork: Pickawoowoo Author Services
Print and Channel Distribution: Lightning Source / Ingram (US/UK/AUS/ EUR)

Publisher: Uma Publishing Group
www.umapublishing.com

Dedication

This book is dedicated to all children and the friendships they make.

Along the Australian bushland, in the hilly paddocks of Bacchus Marsh, in Victoria, there lived a little wombat called Wayne.

Wayne was small in comparison to all the other wombats. He was also scared and shy.

For this reason, he never went far from his burrow and always played near his wombat home and family.

Wombat Wayne's favourite game was using his nose to dig the soil in front of him.

Whenever he did this, his front paws provided him with the support he needed.

To the other wombats, it seemed like Wombat Wayne was walking with his hind legs up in the air.

He was happy when he did this and always made little songs as he went along.

"Riga, a dig, dig, in the soft soil go! See what you find in the land below," he sang as he dug furiously, throwing bits of soil into the air.

One particular day in winter, Wombat Wayne could not go to sleep like the rest of his family.

The wombat world, you see, normally slept during the day and played at night.

Anyhow, Wayne decided that he would dig and add another bit to his song.

"Riga, dig, dig. I will use my clever nose, so! Then see what's in the land below," he sang.

Suddenly, his nose touched something that was hard. It was a little ball, shaped like an acorn without its top. He began to make a new line for his song, "Riga, dig, dig. I find a ball just so! Down in the land below."

The ball was made up of bright little patches of coloured leather that were sewn together. It was just the right size for him to hold.

Wombat Wayne found that when he held the ball up, the sun began to dance on it. The faster he moved the ball, the more beautiful the colours became.

The colour green became purple, then red and finally orange.

Immediately, Wombat Wayne began to sing. "Riga, dig, dig, up comes a magical acorn ball, so! Down, down there from the land below."

"Let's be friends," Wombat Wayne said to the ball. "And play together always."

So, whenever he could not sleep during the day, Wombat Wayne would come out of his burrow and look for his friend, the acorn-shaped ball.

He would toss the ball up in the air with his nose and then watch it come down. He would bounce it with his nose and then run after it to catch it with both paws.

Sometimes he would stand in front of the ball and kick it backwards with his hind legs and then quickly turn and chase after it as it rolled down the hillside. He kept it hidden in the soil when he finished so that he could play his favourite game of digging at the start of each day.

He was doing that now and found that he could add another line to his song, "I toss, I bounce, I watch it so! Here's my treasure from the land below."

One day something happened that made Wombat Wayne sad. He could not find the little ball that was shaped like an acorn.

Wombat Wayne searched under the Lilly Pilli tree. He looked inside the big trunk folds, but the ball was not there.

He tried to sing because he thought singing would make him happy and it might help him find the ball.

But he found that he could not do that because he was unhappy.

He ran a few yards into the leaves of the Pig Face flower. He searched between its pink and red flowers but he could not find the ball.

He found himself getting lost in it too.

But no, the little ball that was of rainbow colours and was shaped like an acorn was nowhere to be seen.

"Where could it be?" wondered Wombat Wayne. "I do so want my playmate and I do so want to sing! It makes me happy."

He was so worried that he began to ask around. "Have you seen a little ball shaped like an acorn?" he asked Koree the kookaburra.

"No, but I could fly up this tall beech tree and look for its colours. Then I'd know where it is."

Koree the kookaburra flew up and around but had to come back and tell Wombat Wayne that he had not found the ball. Wayne thanked him and continued his search.

Next Wombat Wayne asked Matilda the kangaroo. "Mother Matilda, have you seen my little ball that looks like an acorn of many colours?"

"Nope, but I'll see if my older joey has put it in my pouch." Mother Matilda dug with her front paws into her pouch but all she came up with was a tiny baby kangaroo shaped like a jellybean. "Nope it's just my little baby joey in here," she said. Wayne thanked Mother Matilda and continued on his search.

Wombat Wayne hurried away on his little legs. He was getting worried.

In the tall grass, he saw his friend Eka the emu. "Could you help me please? I have lost my little ball.

It looks like an acorn and has lots of colours," he said tearfully.

I'll see if it is amongst our eggs," Eka said. He carefully moved his claw around the large blue eggs.

"No….oo, it's not here. Sorry." Noticing Wombat Wayne's unhappy face, he said, "Hey, look do you want to see my chicks come out? They are beginning to hatch now."

"Thanks, Eka but another time. Gotta go," Wombat Wayne turned at a run, and hurried away.

"I'll ask my Dad's friend, Patrick the platypus and then I'll just have to go home," he muttered to himself. Wombat Wayne ran as fast as he could to the nature reserve that was beside his little burrow. There he found Patrick, the platypus, on the far side of a grassy bank. "Mr Patrick, have you seen a ball shaped like an acorn? It has many colours, and it is mine." By now Wombat Wayne was feeling extremely sad.

"No, I haven't but I'll dive into the lake, if you like and see if it's there." Patrick, the platypus slid down the bank and dived deep down into the still waters of Corioville Sanctuary. He came up a few minutes later carrying an algae-covered plastic slipper. "This is all I saw," he said. "This lake is pretty clean."

"Well thanks anyway," replied Wombat Wayne. "I had better hurry home now."

When Wayne got home, his mother was very worried. "Where have you been?" she said. "I almost had a wombat search party out for you!"

"I was out looking for my ball. You know, the one shaped like an acorn. Have you seen it?"

"Of course, I have," Mother Wombat replied. "There it is, high up in the eucalyptus tree. Young Joey Koalakin has it. See, he is sitting there with Mama Akashi and Grandfather Kashy."

Wombat Wayne looked up and as sure as wombat hair, there was his ball that was shaped like an acorn high up in the tree.

Young Joey Koalakin was smiling and holding it in his paw.

Young Joey Koalakin looked down. "Is this yours?" he said. "I saw it glistening in the grass and wanted to have a closer look at it. Here, you can have it back. But can I play with it sometimes?"

"Of course, you can," replied Wombat Wayne taking the ball. As he hurried away, as happy as a wombat can be, his song came back to him with another new line.

"Yes, yes, yes!"

Wombat Wayne found that he could remember his whole song perfectly now. He began to sing.

Suddenly, he stopped singing and said to himself, "Hey, I never thought I could do this! I'm not scared. I've talked to so many animals today. They are not just animals; they are my friends! I am going to invite my friends to a party and sing to them."

At the party, Wombat Wayne gave a little speech. He said, "My friends, you along with my acorn ball, have become my true mates. You have helped me conquer my shyness and fear. I would like to sing you my new song." Wombat Wayne then began to sing.

"Riga, dig, dig, in the soft soil I go!
See what I find in the land below.
Dig with my nose and dig with my toe!
To see what's in the land below.
Riga, dig, dig, I find a ball just so!
Down, down there in the land below.
Riga, dig, dig, up comes a magical acorn!
I toss, I bounce, I watch it so!
Here's my treasure from the land below.
For me to play with my friends. Yes, yes, yes!"

Wayne's friends gave a loud cheer, exclaiming with happiness,
"Hurrah to Wayne the Wombat. He is a true friend too."

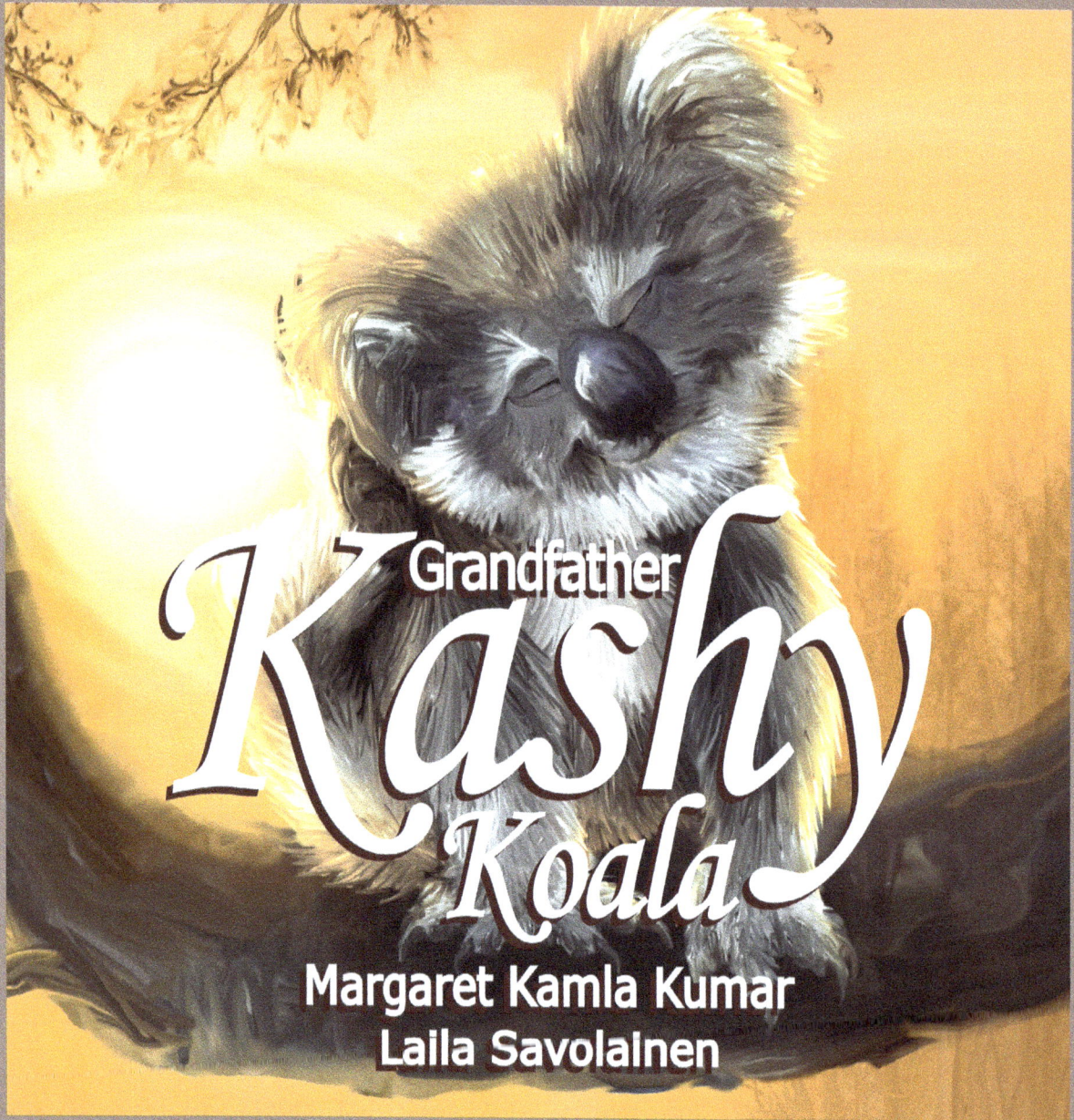

Grandfather
Kashy
Koala

Margaret Kamla Kumar
Laila Savolainen

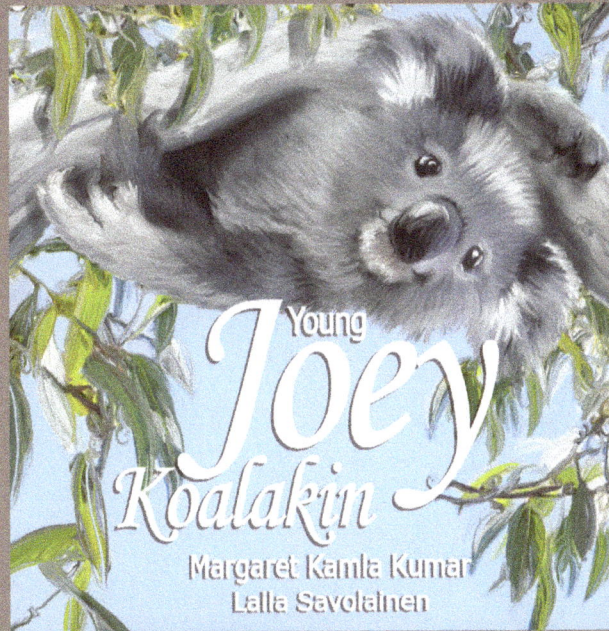

Young
Joey
Koalakin

Margaret Kamla Kumar
Laila Savolainen

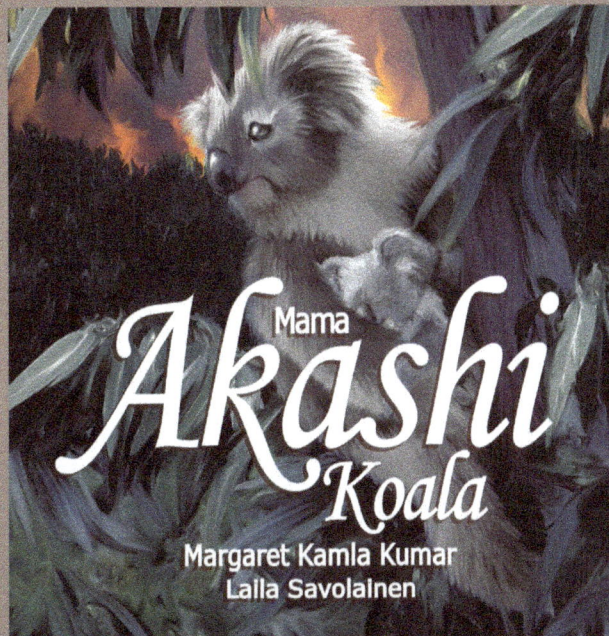

Mama
Akashi
Koala

Margaret Kamla Kumar
Laila Savolainen

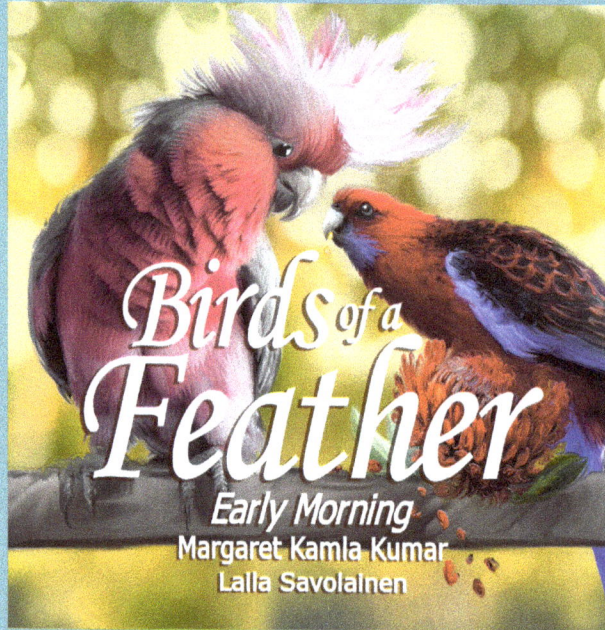

Birds *of a* **Feather**
Early Morning
Margaret Kamla Kumar
Laila Savolainen

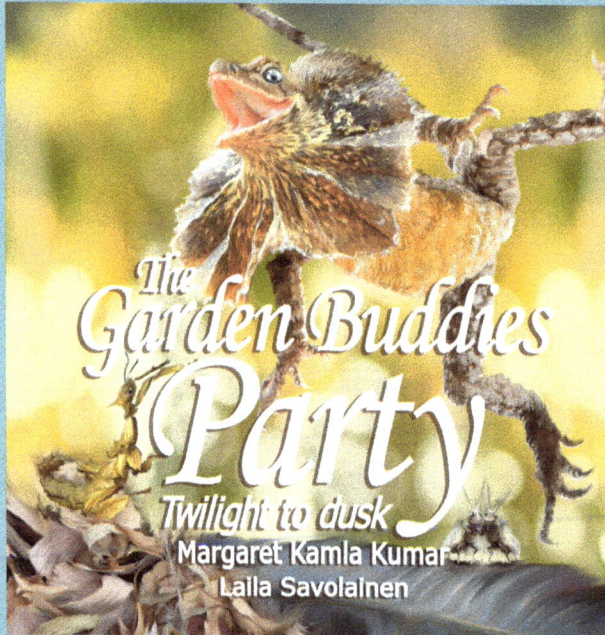

The **Garden Buddies Party**
Twilight to dusk
Margaret Kamla Kumar
Laila Savolainen

36

www.ingramcontent.com/pod-product-compliance
Lightning Source LLC
Chambersburg PA
CBHW051557030426
42334CB00034B/3472